SIR JOHN A

SIR JOHN A

Acts of a Gentrified Ojibway Rebellion

A PLAY BY

Drew Hayden Taylor

Talonbooks

Talonbooks
278 East First Avenue, Vancouver, British Columbia, Canada V5T 1A6
talonbooks.com

Talonbooks is located on xʷməθkʷəy̓əm, Sḵwx̱wú7mesh, and səlilwətaʔɬ Lands.

First printing: 2018

Typeset in Arno
Printed and bound in Canada on 100% post-consumer recycled paper

Cover design by Cara Bain
Interior design by Typesmith

Talonbooks acknowledges the financial support of the Canada Council for the Arts, the Government of Canada through the Canada Book Fund, and the Province of British Columbia through the British Columbia Arts Council and the Book Publishing Tax Credit.

Rights to produce *Sir John A: Acts of a Gentrified Ojibway Rebellion*, in whole or in part, in any medium by any group, amateur or professional, are retained by the author. Interested persons are requested to contact Janine Cheeseman, Aurora Artists Agency, 19 Wroxeter Avenue, Toronto, Ontario, M4K 1J5; TELEPHONE: 416-463-4634; FAX: 416-463-4889; EMAIL: aurora.artists@sympatico.ca.

LIBRARY AND ARCHIVES CANADA CATALOGUING IN PUBLICATION

Taylor, Drew Hayden, 1962–, author
     Sir John A : acts of a gentrified Ojibway rebellion / by
Drew Hayden Taylor.

A play.
ISBN 978-1-77201-214-9 (SOFTCOVER)

     I. Title. II. Title: Acts of a gentrified Ojibway rebellion.

PS8589.A885S57 2018   C812'.54   C2018-903322-3

Thanks to Janine who has dealt with the ups and downs of living with a writer.

PREFACE

What a ride. It all began with a Skype call from Jillian Keiley, English Theatre Artistic Director at the National Arts Centre (NAC) in Ottawa. I was sitting at the kitchen table on my Reserve, curious as to why she wanted to talk to me. I soon learned: Canada 150 was fast approaching and the NAC was feeling obligated to do something about our founding prime minister. While I can't speak for Ms. Keiley, I got the impression the NAC didn't want to do yet another straight biography of Macdonald – somewhere along the line, she'd come up with the idea of telling his story through the eyes of the Indigenous community that he so traumatized via his policies. And that's how I came into the picture.

Truth be told, I was puzzled at the offer. I wasn't exactly known for writing about dead White politicians, and I wasn't known for writing a lot of historical drama, either. I was a humourist who occasionally forayed into dramatic storytelling. But Jillian Keiley convinced me I could do it and, more importantly, that it should be done. (Who was I to argue with an artistic director of the NAC?) So I read and I read and I read about the man. Contrary to popular belief, Canadian history is not boring. There was a lot of fun and drama dripping off our first prime minister. But how to tackle it?! What would be my unique spin? As a fellow playwright is wont to say, "Aye, there's the rub!"

Then I remembered a story an Elder from my Reserve had told me some years back. Two Indigenous guys, he said, decided to jump into a car, drive to Kingston, dig up the bones of Sir John A., and hold them for a ransom of some kind. The tale was sort of an urban legend or, in our case, a Rez legend. The more it bounced around in my head, the more the story I was going to write took shape.

As I wrote, I began to feel that the tone of the story could use some fun music, something that reflected the nature and world of one particular character. So I started throwing songs in, exchanging the pronoun "you" for a character named "Hugh" – I am all for a fun-loving, egocentric goofball who steals the show. From there, the play just wrote itself.

Be warned: It's a multifaceted kind of play. You could say *Sir John A: Acts of a Gentrified Ojibway Rebellion* is a historical, musical, comedic, biographical, political piece of theatre. A little of something for everybody. I hope you enjoy it as much as me and the people who worked on it did.

Who knew dead White politicians could be so much fun!

—DREW HAYDEN TAYLOR
Curve Lake First Nation

NOTE

For those sharp of eye and knowledgeable about my work, you will no doubt have noticed this is not Bobby Rabbit's first foray into theatre. He first appeared in my play *alterNatives* many years ago. When I was putting together the nuts and bolts for *Sir John A*, it occurred to me this was exactly the kind of battle an older Bobby from *alterNatives* would relish. It's so rare you get to visit your favourite characters later in life.

PRODUCTION HISTORY

Sir John A: Acts of a Gentrified Ojibway Rebellion was first produced at the Azrieli Studio by NAC English Theatre in Ottawa, Canada, from October 3 to 14, 2017, with the following cast and crew:

BOBBY Rabbit	Darrell Dennis
HUGH	Herbie Barnes
ANYA	Katie Ryerson
SIR JOHN A. Macdonald	Martin Julien

Directed by Jim Millan

Set and costumes designed by Anna Treusch

Lighting designed by Martin Conboy

Video designed by Nick Bottomley

Music composed by Moe Berg

Stage managed by Erin Finn, with the assistance of Hilary Nichol as Apprentice Stage Manager

CHARACTERS

BOBBY Rabbit – Indigenous man, forty-ish; a little angry at the world and wants to show it

HUGH – Indigenous man, a little younger; trying to find himself in the world

ANYA – A young woman, university dropout, bright and opinionated

SIR JOHN A. Macdonald – First Prime Minister of Canada

SETTING

The play starts off on an unnamed First Nation north of Toronto, then gradually moves east toward Ontario's Highway 401 (otherwise known as the Macdonald–Cartier Freeway), ending up in a graveyard in Kingston, Ontario.

TIME

Now and then.

Act One

SCENE ONE

*Lights up on a late-nineteenth-century
study. SIR JOHN A. Macdonald enters
the room. For a few seconds he scans a
bookcase; then he pours himself a glass of
sherry. Finally, he addresses the audience.*

SIR JOHN
Indians are strange people. I don't know if you know any.
At one time they can be sullen and quiet, at other times,
angry and vengeful, rarely with any explanation. Truly
a perplexing people. It follows logically of course, what
with their nature and existence being forged from this
intemperate and frequently quarrelsome land. I myself
have encountered them on many occasions – in my
adolescence, my practice as a lawyer, and later as their
prime minister. In fact, as I recall, my last criminal trial
as a lawyer involved defending an Indian. Mohawk, from
one of their nearby communities. When was that ... back
in '39 I believe.

The fellow was charged with a violent murder, though
I am unfamiliar with nonviolent murders. There had
been some altercation one night where my client was
accused of stabbing another Mohawk. Indians being
Indians I suppose. Personally I was quite sure the man
was responsible but, as his lawyer, my opinion as to the
man's guilt was irrelevant. I argued, quite brilliantly if I do
say so myself, that the house where the crime took place

had been far too dark for anybody to be sure who was the actual assailant or what had exactly happened. The Crown just assumed it was my client.

Music rises in the background.

A little legal razzle-dazzle in the right place and I turned a murder charge into a simple manslaughter conviction, resulting in a paltry six months in jail. Ah, sometimes I miss those days.

A chorus of "uh huh" rises in the
background. Lights come up on HUGH
in another part of the stage.

The same razzle-dazzle still happens in Parliament, of course, but it's not quite the same. Politicians and murderers, while often sharing a similar dark soul, exercise their intentions differently.

SIR JOHN fades to black. Silhouetted in
a very rock star–like pose, is HUGH.

HUGH comes down to the audience,
in full rock-god mode, and sings. The song is
reminiscent of The Romantics' 1980 hit "What
I Like About You," with full and overblown
orchestration, but the lyrics substitute
the word "you" for the name "Hugh."

BOBBY walks across the background.
He notices HUGH and yells:

BOBBY
Hugh! Hugh!

The lights change to reveal reality. HUGH is actually in an average kitchen, caught in his happy place. Like a needle being dragged across a record, HUGH returns to BOBBY's reality.

BOBBY
You were getting a bit loud. Where were you this time?

HUGH
No place special.

BOBBY
Yes, you were. Where? Tell me.

HUGH
(*reluctantly then proudly*) Okay. Standing centre stage at the National Arts Centre, singing my heart out to throngs and throngs of excited and devoted fans. (*gesturing to the audience*) They love me.

BOBBY
Yeah good for you. Don't forget the encore. People like encores. Look, I just dropped in to grab a bite before my meeting. Got anything munchable?

HUGH
Always. I'm pretty sure I got some cheese in there – some ham, moose, and an excellent aged baloney.

BOBBY pulls some stuff out of the fridge and starts making himself a sandwich. HUGH grabs some eggs and goes about making scrambled eggs.

BOBBY

I have a feeling things are going to work out this time,
Hugh. I got a good feeling.

HUGH

Positive thinking. That's good. You have a righteous cause.

BOBBY

Damn right I do. It's my grandfather's medicine bundle.
It doesn't belong there.

HUGH

No, it does not. We can just grumble and complain, as our
Aboriginal heritage has taught us well over the last few
centuries. But I prefer to think positive!

BOBBY

Geez, I hate museums.

HUGH

Native people and museums – now there's a dubious
antagonistic relationship. (*pause*) Ever wonder if scientists
could someday GMO a chicken to produce pre-scrambled
eggs? Could be a great time-saver.

BOBBY

Yeah I guess.

HUGH

Maybe I should be a scientist. There's good money
in that I hear. I could discover planets. Find the cure
for something.

BOBBY

Maybe but you're thirty-seven and only have your high school. Most scientists tend to have all sorts of university backgrounds, and big fancy letters behind their name. It's kind of required.

HUGH

Well, that's kind of elitist. Okay, no scientist then. Have fun at your meeting. Remember, use lots of big words. Lawyers and politicians like that. It impresses them. Try and work "antidisestablishmentarianism" into a sentence.

BOBBY

Will do. After the meeting, I thought I'd go visit my grandpa.

HUGH

That's nice. He'd like that.

BOBBY

Haven't been up there since he died. I've been waiting to have some good news to tell him. What are you up to?

HUGH

Waiting to hear back about that job I applied for. Don't know if house painting is where I can really shine as an individual, you know? They seemed concerned about my Jackson Pollock enthusiasm. But I gotta do something. Scrambled eggs don't grow on trees. Unless the chickens are in the tree I guess. And fall out.

BOBBY doesn't respond.

HUGH

That was a joke. Don't look so serious, Bobby.

BOBBY

But this is serious.

HUGH

I know, but there's serious and then there's serious.
Normally you're "I'm driving on an unfamiliar road
during a snowstorm" serious, but now you've got a sort
of "my new girlfriend's given me a weird rash and now
I'm at the doctor's waiting to find out what kind of rash"
type of serious.

BOBBY

It's the ludicrousness of the situation. I've never even seen
that medicine bundle. That's the real tragedy of it.

HUGH

So that museum ain't listening to you. None of them
do. That's the fight and it's a good fight. (*breaking into
an excellent upper-crust English accent*) I read somewhere
the British Museum took some marbles away from a
kid named Elgin and won't give them back. Don't worry,
you're doing all the right things. (*back to his real voice*)
All the Aboriginal political organizations wrote you their
magic-yet-oddly-impotent letters of support. You just
need the Chief to sign off and you will be an unstoppable
Indigenous political force that will lay waste to official
Museum policy.

BOBBY

First of all, stop it. You know I hate it when you talk like
that. Secondly, I'm a little concerned it will take more than
an unstoppable Indigenous political force to do this.

HUGH
I will have none of that attitude in this house, young man.
You promised your grandfather you'd try, and you have.
And that final push is this afternoon ... When again?

BOBBY
I'm seeing the Chief in an hour. Wanna come?

HUGH
Not really.

BOBBY
She's your sister.

HUGH
Doesn't mean I have to talk to her. She's mean. She used
to undo the nuts on my bike wheels. I'm almost positive
she put the black mould in my basement herself. It's no
wonder she went into politics. I am only obligated to see
her at Christmas and Mom's birthday.

BOBBY
There is absolutely nothing normal about you, is there?

HUGH
Bobby, if you're the definition of the word "normal,"
I want a new dictionary.

BOBBY
I wish I could live in your world.

HUGH
I can build you a cottage.

BOBBY
At least my world's real.

HUGH
Doesn't make it any better. There is a balance in life.
Yvonne knew that.

There is a silence.

HUGH
I'm sorry. Did I accidentally kick you in the nads with
that comment?

BOBBY
Friends don't make comments like that to other friends.

HUGH
Sure they do. If you get bit by a rattlesnake, who's willing
to suck out the poison? A complete stranger or a friend?
And I have been detecting a fair amount of poison the last
few months.

BOBBY
I hate your metaphors. We're talking about my
grandfather's medicine pouch and your sister. Can we
stay on topic?

HUGH
No problem. Go to your meeting, Bobby. Got my fingers
crossed for you. If this world has any justice left in it – and
I realize the irony of a Native person saying that – you
should be able to convince my sister, our beloved Chief,
and the Band lawyer to support you in getting back your
grandfather's medicine pouch from that faraway place.
How can they refuse you?

BOBBY
Thanks.

BOBBY exits and HUGH collects the plates.

HUGH
(*singing softly*)
What I like about Hugh ...

*As HUGH exits, he poses in rock god
silhouette as we hard cut to SIR JOHN.*

SCENE TWO

*Light comes up on SIR JOHN in
another area of the stage.*

SIR JOHN
Indians ... I have long struggled with what to do with
them. Truly, they are like children in many ways, simple
and in need of strong direction. Canada has little room
for Indians as they exist now. We are an expanding and
vibrant people. I do not get the impression they are
interested in seeing what we can make of this great nation.
Instead, they hold on to their outdated traditions. Though
I have tried, I do not understand them.

I ask you, isn't it better to have some fine British tea then
to feast on a half-cooked frog? No, it's best we show them
the way like we would any other lost and helpless ward
of our country. I have put into effect policies that will
educate them. That will feed them ... to a certain extent.

One of the responsibilities of being a good parent is showing your children ambition. A half-filled stomach can accomplish a lot more than a sated one. Heaven forbid they should get fat and complacent on Canada's dime.

I think this is a better way than how the Americans handle their Indian problem. Their answer to everything down there is bullets and sabres. I believe they shoot more Indians than buffalo. But Canada is not like that; we are a kind and gentle nation. I say we are gentle and charitable because we are not Americans.

Now quite recently I read this startling book by a man named Darwin. It's taking all the universities and scholars by storm. The author hypothesizes about how every living thing under creation is shaped and developed by outside pressures. Those that can adapt best to a changing environment survive and prosper. Those that cannot, do not.

> Lights up on HUGH sitting at a
> picnic table, listening to music.

We shall try as best we can to assist these people as we fast approach the twentieth century. If left to their own interests, God knows what foolishness these Indians would get into.

> Light goes to black on SIR JOHN as
> BOBBY approaches HUGH.

HUGH
There's the man. How'd it go? Do you know the Canadian government is looking for astronauts? For that space station thing. I'm thinking of applying.

BOBBY
Your sister is a bitch.

HUGH
Yeah I know. How'd the meeting go?

BOBBY
How do you think it went?! They said no. They said
it was complicated. Might screw up all the Canada 150
celebrations. "We don't want to give people the wrong
impression about our enthusiasm." They said I was being
too aggressive, too provocative on purpose. Of course I
am being too provocative on purpose. That's how you get
things done. And get this, our own lawyer said it would
be too catastrophic if museums gave back everything
they took. What the fuck do we care if it's catastrophic to
museums? Wasn't it catastrophic to us when they took my
grandfather's medicine bundle?!

HUGH
Oh Bobby, I'm so sorry. I thought for sure she would help.
My grandfather used to say that every thousand years even
the Devil would do a good deed. I thought for sure she
was due ... Now, about me being the first Indian in space ...

BOBBY
You're too late. I think the Americans had one up there
already. The Space Station still smells of sweetgrass.

HUGH
Ah damn it. So much for that. And I refuse to believe
Canada is 150 years old. Canada is ageless. She has no
beginning and no end. She was here way before we were
and will live on long after we're gone.

BOBBY

Yes. A lot of people in this country don't think this is
worth celebrating.

HUGH

It's more than a celebration. It's a serious party. I believe
there is a big barbeque planned. Some boat races.
My sister is giving a speech. T-shirts. Lots of money being
thrown around. I would have thought your cultural centre
would have been in the thick of things.

BOBBY

Like I would pay attention to all that bullshit. This is not
culture. It's the opposite of culture. It's ... it's cultural
expropriation. Seriously, do you think we should be
celebrating colonization!? Do you realize how many
horrible things this so-called Canada has done to
Aboriginal people? It's insulting and highly offensive.

HUGH

Bobby, it's a barbeque and boat races. I think our ancestors
will survive the insult.

BOBBY

Bigger picture, Hugh. Bigger picture. July 1, 1867. John
A. Macdonald and his grand achievement. And what do
we Native people have to celebrate? Residential schools.
The Indian Act. The Scoop up. Reserves. Sacred things in
museums. Diabetes ...

HUGH

They did give us air-conditioning and KFC.

BOBBY pauses for a moment.

BOBBY
Yes, they did but that doesn't make up for everything.
Your average Canadian is celebrating everything Canada
has given them while we are still dealing with everything
Canada took away. John A. came. John A. saw. John A.
created a country. One that already had lots and lots of
people already living there, practising their own forms
of government and laws. He didn't create a whole new
country ... he regifted a country.

HUGH
(*speaking in a clichéd Indian accent*) Wise words spoken,
my brother. But like a little pine needle floating on the
water, we are at the mercy of the mighty river. (*speaking in
a normal voice*) Or in other words, what are you going to
do? You can't fight the Band Office. The barbeque will be
nice. All-you-can-eat hot dogs. And hey, we can pair up for
the two-man canoe marathon. Bet we kick ass.

*BOBBY seems deep in thought
before making a decision.*

BOBBY
No, ah ... No. Hugh, I'm feeling a bit ... stressed out. Yeah,
I need to do something. Yeah, I need ... a vacation.

HUGH
Bobby, I couldn't agree more. A little vacation would do
you good. So where are you going to go? The Caribbean?
Mexico. Or someplace exotic like Florida?

BOBBY
Kingston.

HUGH
Cool. Kingston, Jamaica ... (*speaking with a
Jamaican accent*) Hey mon, say hello to all the
Buffalo Soldiers for me.

BOBBY
Kingston, Ontario.

HUGH
An odd choice for a vacation but whatever bakes
your bannock.

BOBBY
And you're coming with me.

HUGH
I am? I don't need a vacation. And I don't want to go to
Kingston. I've been to Kingston. The novelty wore off
really quick.

BOBBY
I need you to come with me. For two reasons.

HUGH
These had better be solid gold, ironclad, damn good
reasons. I'm talking free hot dogs for a whole day.

BOBBY
Those hot dogs are laced with racism. The potato salad,
seasoned with colonialism. So, reason one: You need this
trip as much as I do.

HUGH
Do not.

BOBBY

There is a world beyond hot dogs. Hugh, where
do you live?

HUGH

Here.

BOBBY

Where exactly is here?

HUGH

This Reserve.

BOBBY

Right. Three thousand two hundred square acres of land,
owned by the federal government, supposedly for our
benefits. Your Granny Esther and your Grandpa Albert.
Where did they go to school?

HUGH

The residential school up at ...

BOBBY

When did we, the original inhabitants of this country, get
the right to vote?

HUGH

1960.

BOBBY

When did all this start? The whole big shitbox about being
Native? Obligations. Rights. Responsibilities ...

HUGH

Confederation I guess. The Indian Act followed shortly
after that, which begat the Reserve system, which begat
the residential schools, which begat ...

BOBBY

Exactly.

HUGH

"Exactly" ... What exactly is that "exactly" in reference to?

BOBBY

You know this stuff but you don't know this stuff.
Perspective. You need perspective.

HUGH

And I can find this perspective ... in Kingston, huh?

BOBBY

Oh yeah, you'll love it. The irony alone will
make you laugh.

HUGH

Uh huh. And what's the second reason?

BOBBY

I've just had the rug pulled out from underneath me.
By your sister. I need to regroup. I need to develop a new
battle plan. And who knows, it might be fun. You like fun.
And you're my friend. And friends don't let friends go
alone to Kingston.

HUGH

I hate it when you pretend to be human. Goddamn it, I'm
going to Kingston.

BOBBY
You'll find it's a lot more interesting to live a story than to just tell a story. We'll leave first thing in the morning. Now I'm off to the graveyard to see my grandpa.

BOBBY exits and HUGH gathers his things together into his backpack.

HUGH
Kingston?! Fuck!

SCENE THREE

Lights up on SIR JOHN sitting at his desk – he is signing important papers, etc. He continues with this work as he talks to the audience.

SIR JOHN
I was five when we Macdonalds came to this country. Had no idea where we were going or what to expect. Father said we were going and so we went. We left everything we knew in Glasgow and spent weeks aboard a ship that I swear to God, the only thing that kept it together and not sinking was our prayers. Seven of us arrived in Quebec City, after a steady diet of porridge and molasses that even the rats thought was beneath them. People talk of the nostalgia of youth. My nostalgia consists of memories of lice, seasickness, and dampness. It's like becoming Canadian required some form of penance.

After another four weeks travelling up river, sometimes by sail, other times pulled by oxen or men like my father, the hamlet of Kingston appeared along the far shore and became our new home. Some would call the town ... quaint, approximately four thousand people consisting mostly of army personnel, sailors, drunkards, and prostitutes. Ah, welcome to Canada.

Why here, I thought. Why had our father brought us to this semi-civilized land so far away? The Empire had so many other colonies that might be considered a wee bit more promising and inviting. Australia ... though at that time I had not heard the name but still, there is no way on God's green Earth that it could contain more mosquitoes and deer flies than Kingston that August 1820. Same I thought with New Zealand. South Africa, India ... For the first time and not the last time, I wondered if God did indeed have a cruel sense of humour.

Light fades on SIR JOHN as lights come up on BOBBY and HUGH in a car. BOBBY is enjoying the music.

HUGH
Heard from Yvonne?

BOBBY
(*pause*) Yeah, she's busy doing her thing.

There is an awkward silence in the car.

HUGH
It's okay to miss her, you know.

BOBBY

I will keep that in mind.

HUGH

She'd know how to deal with all this museum and bundle stuff. She'd have ideas, and then more ideas, and afterward, come up with a few more. You two were good together. She was one smart cookie, though I don't usually associate intelligence with baked goods. Not that you're not smart, I mean you hooked up my Netflix and all. But she was different.

BOBBY

Yes, she was. She was. That's why she left and we'll just have to make do without her. Think you'll survive?

HUGH

It's not me I'm worried about. So what wonderful relaxing things do you have for us to do in wonderful, downtown Kingston? That's why we're going there, right? That's what you said.

BOBBY

About that … Pop quiz, Hugh. What do you know about Sir John A. Macdonald?

HUGH

Him again? Well, according to grade six history, he was our – and by "our" I mean Canada's – first prime minister. He had a fondness for alcohol and appearing on money. You do know he doesn't live in Kingston anymore. I believe he's dead now.

BOBBY
Yes, he's very much dead. That's why we're going.
Museums all over the world have items stolen from
Aboriginal burial grounds. So, as a form of social
commentary, we my friend are fighting back.

HUGH
Good to know. How?

BOBBY
We, my friend, are going to dig Sir John A up and hold his
bones for ransom. Smart, huh?

> For a second HUGH doesn't respond. He is
> processing everything BOBBY has told him.

BOBBY
Now I know you're probably a little surprised, maybe
even a little upset. I understand that. And you're probably
thinking that this isn't exactly legal but we're two Native
men battling against an unjust and racist society. "Legal"
is a debatable term.

HUGH
No, it's not and let me out of this stupid car. NOW! You
stupid, crazy, insane ...

> He opens the door of his car as it's
> still in motion and BOBBY has to
> move quickly to pull the car over.

> HUGH angrily exits the vehicle. BOBBY follows.

BOBBY
Jesus, Hugh ... Look, I know you're a little ...

HUGH
LITTLE? LITTLE? This is exactly why Yvonne left. This is
exactly why everybody leaves you. I would say you were
an insane idiot but that would be giving insane idiots a
bad name. Dig up Sir John A. Macdonald's bones! That
is ... You are ... Oh God I'm hyperventilating. Christ it's
going to be a long walk back home.

BOBBY
Hugh, just listen to me for a second ...

HUGH
I didn't have to get in the car. I could have just stood
in front of it and said, "Why not just run me over?"
It would be quicker.

BOBBY
Hugh, focus. Let me explain ...

HUGH
Oh Bobby, by all means, do explain. If I am going to spend
an entire day committing what I assume is a major crime,
and then the rest of my life in jail, I would love to have
some sort of explanation to tell my lawyer.

BOBBY
Think of us as modern-day archaeologists. Caucasiana
Jones and the Grave of the Colonizer. We're going there
to make a political point that has ramifications for all First
Nations people across this land. They steal our sacred
items. We steal theirs.

HUGH
Indian see, Indian do. That's not exactly a valid
defence strategy.

BOBBY

Come on. Social protest. Political disobedience. It will be like it was back in the '60s.

HUGH

You were born in '78. And why did I have to come with you? This is serious, you know. I've got nothing against these people. Some of my best friends are White. Besides, you think we hate it when they dig up our ancestors? White people hate it even more. We protest. They throw people in jail. They'll throw *us* in jail. Bad bad bad bad!

BOBBY pauses for a moment.

BOBBY

With that kind of defeatist attitude, sure. But what are two more Native people in the prison system? I doubt people would notice. Come on, Hugh, you're my buddy. My pal.

HUGH

I'm scared for you, Bobby. You've flown off the handle before but seriously, these are federal laws you'll be breaking. The minute that shovel hits the dirt, you just may end up sharing a cell with what could become your new boyfriend.

BOBBY

That medicine bundle is probably rotting in some museum basement. It doesn't belong there. It belongs here. I have done everything I could – legally – to get it back. Now I may have to colour outside the lines ... for the medicine bundle and all the other things hoarded away in museums all around the world. Sometimes being Native requires sacrifices. Think of this as our Sun Dance.

HUGH
The Anishnawbe never had the Sun Dance, Bobby.

BOBBY
The point is still relevant.

There is a pause.

BOBBY
Well? (*no response*) Hugh?

HUGH
Every fibre in my body is saying go home, find a rerun of
North of 60 somewhere and forget this day ever began. I'm
getting too old to get pepper-sprayed, Bobby.

BOBBY
But?

HUGH
Who am I to stand in the way of your sojourn of justice?
I did say your cause was just and your grandfather was a
good man. Let's go rock Kingston.

BOBBY
Thanks Hugh. We are going to be a lean, mean,
excavating machine!

They get back in the car.

HUGH
And you wonder why I keep going to my happy place.

SCENE FOUR

*Once again, SIR JOHN is at his desk
working, with a decanter of sherry on
the desk and a half-filled glass.*

SIR JOHN
Over the years as I matured, I saw this little backward town –
reminiscent of the whole country – grow gradually to its
own form of manhood. Like all grown children now absent
from home, we pay our own rent, plan our own future, and
clean up our own messes. Aye, I gave them that. When
Britons speak of Canadians, they speak well. And when
Canadians speak of Britain, we speak of home ... except for
the French, and the Irish, and the Indians and ... I mean real
Canadians. All that really matters, regardless of where I may
be sleeping or pissing or dying: I was born a British subject
and I will die a British subject. God save the Queen.

> *SIR JOHN takes a drink. As lights fade on
> SIR JOHN lights come up on HUGH in a
> McDonald's restaurant. He, with a backpack,
> is singing again, this time "Crazy on You"
> by Heart, still substituting "Hugh" for "you."*

> *Nearby, a young non-Native woman is
> watching HUGH. Her name is ANYA, and
> she seems slightly amused by HUGH's
> shenanigans. She even joins in on the song.*

HUGH
(*singing*)
But go crazy on Hugh
Crazy on Hugh

ANYA
(*singing*)
… on you …

HUGH
(*singing*)
Let me go crazy, crazy on Hugh, Hugh!

ANYA
You?

HUGH
No, Hugh. Hugh. My name is Hugh.

ANYA
Oh your name is Hugh. Got it. Funny. Hello, Hugh.
My name's Anya.

HUGH
Anya, what a beautiful name.

ANYA
Thanks. You a big Heart fan?

HUGH
Who?

ANYA
Heart. That's who sang the song.

HUGH
No. Just like that song.

ANYA
Is that why you sing "Hugh" instead of "you"?

HUGH

Hey, if you aren't the main character in your own musical, what's the point?

ANYA

That's a unique perspective.

HUGH

Yes, it is. You're not the main character in your musical? How sad.

ANYA

I don't have a musical. Not much to sing about.

HUGH

That sounds kind of grumpy.

ANYA

Pissed off is a better way of putting it.

HUGH

Hmm, there's a lot of that going around these days. Do tell.

It takes a second for ANYA to decide if she's going to share her story.

ANYA

Okay. I just broke up with my partner. I don't have any money on me. And I am marooned at a roadside McDonald's.

HUGH

Sounds like a country song. So why are you marooned at a McDonald's with no money?

ANYA

Because I dated an asshole ...

HUGH

I think it's safe to say we've all dated assholes at one time
or another.

ANYA

Well, my personal asshole lives up near Parry Sound, and
that's how I ended up here.

There is an awkward silence.

HUGH

You don't usually think of Parry Sound as an assholey
kind of town.

ANYA

I think they breed up there. This is not how I thought
my week would end. Okay, we were at Chris's family's
cottage – that's the asshole. I thought this would be a good
chance to really get to know each other, you know? We've
only been going out about three months or so and this
was going to be some quality alone time. I had envisioned
a deeply romantic weekend looking deep into each other's
eyes and plumbing the depths of our souls.

HUGH

Oh no ... Let me guess. Chris didn't have any
depth or soul.

ANYA

I didn't get that far. Basically as we lay there in front of this
gorgeous fireplace Chris found it rather important to tell
me that whatever may happen with us down the road, not

to expect any marriage or kids. That wasn't part of the big picture, I was told. That was bad enough but ... but ... get this ... every five years we would reassess our relationship and see if it was worth continuing. That's a thing now!

HUGH

Five years! Wow!

ANYA

Yeah! Can you believe it? I threw my wine glass and hit some piss-poor reproduction of one of those Group of Seven painters and just stormed out. Problem is, my former squeeze muffin drove us up and I left my purse with all my money and cards somewhere up in the cottage bedroom. Thus my current state of abandonment at this McDonald's.

HUGH

And zero interest in going back and getting your purse?

ANYA

Everything – and I mean everything – I left in that cottage is replaceable. I just got to figure out how to get to Kingston.

HUGH

Ah, you're Kingston-bound.

ANYA

That's where I live. I have a feeling it's going to be a long and embarrassing day of car-hopping, with a high probability of creeps harassing me along the way. I don't even know if hitchhiking is legal anymore. Do people still use their thumbs, or do I need to make a cardboard sign?

> *BOBBY approaches them carrying*
> *a big bag of fast food to go.*

BOBBY
Okay, got everything. Let's get back on the road.

HUGH
Hey Bobby, meet Anya.

BOBBY
Hi Anya. Let's get going, Hugh.

HUGH
Anya's going to Kingston.

BOBBY
Yeah?

HUGH
Anya, we're going to Kingston. What a coinkydink, huh?!
I think we should give her a ride. Don't you think, Bobby?

ANYA
What? With the two of you ...

BOBBY
Uh Hugh, we have so much to do and ... this might
complicate things and I ...

HUGH
What complications? Come on, she can join us on our
great sojourn of justice across this great province. She can
be our faithful White guide.

ANYA
Thank you but ...

HUGH
But what?

Awkward silence.

ANYA
Yes, I've been sitting here for hours trying to get a ride.
The closest I got was a guy offering to buy me an Egg
McMuffin, and he put a little too much emphasis on the
"muffin" part, if you know what I mean. Still ... and no
offence guys, I haven't the vaguest idea who you two are.

BOBBY
You heard the lady, Hugh. We're dangerous and psychotic
men. Let's go before your McNuggets get cold.

HUGH
Bobby, is it in the warrior tradition to leave behind a lost
and defenseless woman, trapped forever in a McDonald's,
like in some Greek legend? (*quietly*) I do crazy insane
things for you; you have to do the occasional one for
me. Friends don't let friends not be friends to other
potential friends.

BOBBY
Fine then. We need gas. Meet me at the gas bar.

He shoves the food into HUGH's
hands and exits.

HUGH
We will meet you at the gas bar. And you, young lady,
yes we are two mysterious men. But all you need to
know is Bobby's bark is worse than his bite, and I'm ...
essentially ... adorable. Now you can stay here, trapped for
eternity smelling of French fry grease, or get a ride directly
to downtown Kingston. Where should we drop you off?

ANYA
Near Queens. I live just off campus. I just want to get
home and away from all this insanity. Normally I live a
depressingly quiet and sane life.

HUGH
You too?!

ANYA
Hugh, no offence but just to let you know, I have a big
knife, just in case ... you know ...

HUGH
Oh good. I just bought some peanut butter and crackers.
We can use your big knife to spread the peanut butter.

> ANYA *is still hesitating and*
> *looking uncomfortable.*

ANYA
Thanks but ...

HUGH
Here, maybe this will help. Just a second ...

> HUGH *pulls a spray can out of his*
> *backpack and gives it to* ANYA.

HUGH

This might make you feel a little safer.

ANYA

(*taking it*) Bear spray. Why do you have a can
of bear spray?

HUGH

(*confused*) To ... spray ... bears. I didn't realize that
was such a leap of logic. There's a lot of bears where
we come from.

> ANYA *is weighing things and finally relents.*

ANYA

Well, can't argue with bear spray, and I am
rather desperate.

HUGH

Perfect. Desperate and me are old friends. Isn't it amazing
how things just work out? Let's go.

> *They exit, with HUGH not getting the relevance
> of ANYA's comment, or choosing to ignore it.*

SCENE FIVE

> *SIR JOHN is once again sitting in his study.
> At each appearance he should be getting
> drunker and gradually complaining more.*

SIR JOHN

Americans. If you listen closely, you can hear them breathing, lusting, just across yon border. Gazing northward at us like sailors at some virginal young woman crossing the street. The only thing that keeps them at bay is our winter and our resolve. They are Napoleon to our Russia. Some of my compatriots think I am being too critical in my thinking. I mean, as individuals, they are fine and excellent people. I canna say otherwise. But I dare say we can hear their expansionistic bellies start grumbling. And Canada be a nice succulent yearling lamb in their eyes. Now don't get me wrong, I have been south of our polite border many times. It is a fine country.

When I was young, having been in this country only a handful of years, there was a family in Kingston that lived across the way. Also from Scotland. The Bairds. Fine, hardworking, God-fearing people. Over the years our two families would frequently meet. My father was even known to throw back a glass or two with Old Man Baird. Many said they had their share of faults. It was said the elder Baird had a bad habit of telling people how they should live their lives. The wife was a little too pious and not afraid to rain down hellfire on those she felt needed it. And the children, all too rowdy and mischievous for anybody's tastes.

But who amongst us hasn't been born with flaws. Aye, we were made in God's image but occasionally that image blurred. But ... and here's the important part, they were the Bairds and we were the Macdonalds. We were not them, and they were not us. Same with these Americans. It's my belief Americans make great Americans but poor Canadians.

I'm sure some may view us as squabbling siblings, as we were both born from the same mother, our glorious England. But our childhoods were somewhat different. While we good Canadians were happy to nestle and grow at the teat of one of the greatest and most cultured empires to ever shine on God's green Earth, our big brother America saw fit to rip the whole tit right off during their Revolutionary War. Their history has been written in blood while ours has been written in commerce. They are bold while we are diplomatic. Their emblem is an eagle while ours is a beaver. And eagles can eat beavers.

No, it is good we have a definable and legal border between our two nations. I like Americans. Even more importantly, I like Americans ... over there. Over the years I lost touch with the Bairds. I did hear a rumour some time ago that the entire family moved south, seeking their fortune. Maybe the Americans will know what to do with them. (*taking a drink*) Fucking Bairds.

> *SIR JOHN exits. BOBBY and HUGH
> are in the front seat of the car. ANYA is
> in the back looking out the window.*

ANYA

Holstein ... Brown Swiss ... and some Devons. God I hate cows.

HUGH

That's awfully judgmental. What did they ever do to you?

ANYA

Grew up around them. Got milk in my veins. My parents wanted me to take part in their bovine empire. But the idea of spending my life running the dairy farm just did not appeal to me. Ever spent time with cows? They're gooey. There's goo coming from practically every part of them. I long ago passed my goo tolerance.

HUGH
Fascinating. Goo.

ANYA
You know, I think I'm just too damn trusting. I trusted Chris. Look what happened. Now I'm in a car with two guys I've never met.

HUGH
Well, a few hours at a McDonald's can make you do stupid things.

ANYA
So it seems. I take it you guys are First Nations.

BOBBY
And what makes you say that?

HUGH
The way we talk? Our complexion? My fabulous sense of humour? Bobby's stoic personality? The faint aroma of muskrat in the car?

ANYA
The dreamcatcher hanging from the rear-view mirror. So what is bringing you two guys to the big city of Kingston? Other than that justice sojourn thing of yours.

HUGH and BOBBY look at each other.

HUGH

Well, since you asked. We plan, by action, to comment through civil disobedience ...

BOBBY

Hugh ...

HUGH

... on several wrongs perpetrated by the Canadian government and other associate governments and organizations, and by doing that ...

BOBBY

Hugh ...

HUGH

... hopefully rectify a series of oppressive issues experienced by the Native people of this land. In a 2006 Kia Sportage to boot.

BOBBY

Hugh, how do you say "shut up" in Anishnawbe?

ANYA

Ooh, I like that. I'm all for a little civil disobedience. So what do you have planned? Something Idle No More-ish? A Round Dance maybe?

BOBBY

Blocking traffic is only so effective in the long run.

HUGH

But you're getting warmer. Hey Bobby, don't you think that was a little ironic? I mean, on our way to Sir John A.

Macdonald's grave and we end up eating at a McDonald's?
Is that karma, irony, coincidence, or serendipity?

BOBBY
More like necessity and the profitability of franchises. And
shut up. Those McNuggets make you talk too much.

HUGH
Ah, you love me. (*to ANYA*) He's so passionate, isn't he?

ANYA
So you're going to visit the big guy himself, huh? Can't
say that I blame you for protesting him. His record on
Native issues wasn't exactly, um, progressive. What you
gotta understand is he was a man of his times, historically
speaking. He was probably no better or worse than the
majority of other men of his era.

BOBBY
My great uncle died in a residential school. Guess that
made him a man of his times too.

ANYA
It's all about context.

BOBBY
I'm sure it is. That forgives a lot. You know much
about Macdonald?

ANYA
Macdonald is just one of my areas of expertise.

BOBBY
Oh really? Do regale us with your expertise.

ANYA

Uh okay ... If it weren't for him, we'd quite probably be
Americans. Middle of the 1800s, Americans were always
talking about annexing Canada. Especially with an
experienced and battle-hardened army, fresh off the Civil
War. Some generals thought it would just be a matter of
boots marching north. That helped precipitate John A.
and his buddies to orchestrate Confederation. Canada
became Canada to avoid being American. Funny, huh?

HUGH

I did not know that. That is kind of funny.

BOBBY

Hilarious. The thing about history, as you have said, is it's
all a matter of perspective. Or context. There's that word
again. And I don't think it really made any difference,
about Canada and America. Can't say the American policy
toward Native people would have been any different. They
shot us. Macdonald tried to absorb or starve us.

ANYA

That's a little harsh.

BOBBY

Sorry. I'm sure in a hundred years people will say I'm a
man of my times too. So try and see me in context.

*In the back, ANYA slumps down in her
seat. There is an awkward silence.*

HUGH

I'm hungry.

BOBBY
We ate half an hour ago.

HUGH
What does eating have to do with being hungry? I believe
I have some crackers and peanut butter somewhere in the
back. Anya, I think it's in my backpack, if you don't mind.

She fishes around for the bag
and hands it to HUGH.

HUGH
Thank you. Any civilization that created peanut butter
can't be all bad, right Bobby?

BOBBY
Actually peanuts were originally grown by South
American Native people, and then developed into peanut
butter by an ex-slave named George Washington Carver.

HUGH
Interesting. The ultimate anti-establishment, anti-colonial
lunch spread. Anya, if you don't mind, you said you
had a knife?

HUGH looks back at her expectantly.
She briefly weighs the decision, and
then hands HUGH a butter knife.

HUGH
This is your big dangerous knife?! I guess if you're a block
of butter. (*ANYA shrugs*) As our people say ... t'anks.

HUGH begins unpackaging everything,
spreading the P.B. on the crackers, and

> *passing them around, but nobody wants*
> *any. He ends up eating all of them.*

BOBBY

Anya, where you from? I mean way back. Where did your family come from?

ANYA

Well, like a lot of Canadians, got a little of everything. Mostly English and Scandinavian, though.

BOBBY

Vikings and the British Empire. Never met a country they didn't want to invade or colonize.

ANYA

(*jokingly*) That's being a little racist, don't you think?

BOBBY

Oh come on, true racism has little to do with race. It's about a power paradigm. About one level of society having more influence and control over another level of society. The races are interchangeable, but the oppression isn't. So in this part of the globe, White privilege rules.

ANYA

Yeah, I know that argument. They say the same thing about rape. Rape isn't about sex; it's about power.

BOBBY

You disagree?

ANYA

About rape, no. About racism, yes. I think it's more complicated. Socio-politically, it's been said, racism only exists from the top down. It's about exclusion, about privilege, the class system. It's a complex attitude with complex exceptions. I've heard some of your snide remarks about White people ... so on its own level, yes, I do believe it is possible that you, a First Nations man, could be racist against me, a middle-class White woman.

> *HUGH offers ANYA a cracker*
> *covered with peanut butter.*

HUGH
Cracker?

ANYA
Yes, thank you.

> *ANYA takes one.*

HUGH
Bobby?

BOBBY
No. (*pause*) Yes.

> *BOBBY takes one.*

HUGH
See Bobby, she's another smart cookie ... A cracker-eating cookie. Hey Bobby, can I ask you a question?

BOBBY
No.

HUGH
Just thinking, how will your plan solve all our problems?

BOBBY
It will be a bargaining chip.

There is silence in the car for a few seconds.

ANYA
Bargaining chip?

HUGH
I'm still having difficulty trying to conceive a happy or
even positive outcome to all this. And while you are
one smart guy, this is kind of outside our level of Rez
school education. Do you even know how to go about
blackmailing the government?

ANYA
Blackmailing?! What's going on here?

BOBBY
I know perfectly well how to handle it. It will be
a fair trade.

HUGH
This is a fair trade?! The bones of Sir John A. Macdonald
for the medicine pouch?!

*ANYA perks up as she hears this. She
grows increasingly concerned.*

ANYA
The bones ... The bones of Sir John A. Macdonald?!

HUGH
Anya, Bobby is on a mission.

BOBBY
We are on a mission. You're part of this equation too.

ANYA
What mission? Give me that!

> *She quickly grabs the knife from HUGH. The knife's still smeared in peanut butter. Noticing the peanut butter, she quickly licks it off to make herself look more ominous. ANYA is armed, with a butter knife, and the bear spray.*

ANYA
I want some answers here! I want some real fucking answers now.

HUGH
Bobby, she wants some real fucking answers. Now.

BOBBY
This is why I never pick up hitchhikers. Christ, I need a drink.

ANYA
Pull over now! PULL OVER! PULL OVER! I've got bear spray.

> *Dialogue should be fast, excited and overlapping.*

HUGH
(*raising his voice*) Hey be careful with that!

BOBBY
(*speaking over*) Where the hell did she get bear spray?
(*toward ANYA*) Don't ... Don't ...

HUGH
I gave it to her.

BOBBY
You gave it to her?! If she sprays that in here ...

ANYA
(*overlapping*) I will use it!

HUGH
But we're not bears!

BOBBY
(*speaking over*) Ah double Christ. I'm pulling over.

    He pulls over.

SCENE SIX

    Back in SIR JOHN's study. SIR JOHN
    is taking a sip of brandy.

SIR JOHN
On occasion, I like a drink. Maybe a few. Brandy if it's
handy. Ale will never fail. Wine can fill any glass of mine.
Sherry if I'm feeling a bit hairy. Gin will make me grin. And
from champagne I will never abstain. People find it a wee
bit odd that I, a good Scotsman with the name Macdonald,

am not a bosom friend of whisky. Aye, it's fine. It will get the job done. But there's something about it that doesn't exactly tickle my fancy. The smoky flavour coming from the peat – like burnt dirt – takes me back to home. Peat, you see, was used to heat many of the houses. We left that behind.

Aye, and I've lost a lot in my journey. My father, a barely competent merchant, forced to Canada, leaving behind sizable debts. My brother James, ah poor James, died at the age five. A blow to the head, killed by a servant (*taking a drink*). And then there was John, the first real Canadian of our family. Barely a year passed before he left Isabella and me. It broke our hearts. (*taking a drink*) I miss you, lad. My first wife, Isabella, bedridden for more than a decade. Now sleeping forever. (*taking a drink*) To you, my Isabella, may you finally be able to dance. And then of course there's Hugh, my headstrong and wilful son. Barely spoken to the boy in years. Ah Hugh, my boy, wish you were here to drink with me. (*taking a drink*) My lovely Mary. No man loved his daughter more, I don't think. Aye, you were born ill. You were different, but it just made you all the more special. I drink to you, my daughter, not out of sadness, but out of joy. May you outlive me, and this new century be as happy as you made me.

(*taking more drinks*) People say I drink too much. I tell them ... I think I don't drink nearly enough.

> *Exit SIR JOHN. BOBBY and ANYA are sitting at a small table in a bar, nursing drafts. HUGH is over by a jukebox looking at songs. He is waving his butt to the sound of the background music.*

ANYA

And you're the genius who came up with this master
plan! You can't do this. Whatever your heritage is doesn't
give you permission to desecrate a grave, let alone one
belonging to the Father of Confederation.

BOBBY

Your father. Not ours. If he is ours then he was more
of an abusive father. Didn't they teach you this stuff
in university?

ANYA

In 1885 he suggested to Parliament that Native people be
given the vote. And not lose their status when they get it.
Didn't they teach you that wherever you came from?

BOBBY

I came from this thing called a Reserve, which he helped
create. He got the ball rolling on the residential school
system. I could go on and on. The crime of digging up
a grave seems pretty paltry compared to all that. It's a
statement we're making.

ANYA

I can't believe I got in the same car with you guys. You
know, we all got our problems. It's not easy being a
woman in this society either.

BOBBY

A middle-class, well-educated White woman. I am sorry if
I don't know all the words to the "White Woman Blues."

ANYA

You're so fucking condescending.

BOBBY

Technically, can an oppressed minority be condescending?
Doesn't condescension have a sense of superiority to it?
Besides, I don't think we're here to play "Who's More
Oppressed?" We'd need somebody who's Black, Asian,
Jewish, and has a Seeing Eye dog.

ANYA

Condescension can be transcultural. Okay, you in your
brilliance manage to dig up the grave of John A. Macdonald.
What exactly will this statement of yours prove?

BOBBY

Maybe that five hundred years of colonization can have
unexpected paybacks. Not everything can be settled and
placated with an apology and a couple of cheques. I have
a T-shirt that says, "That which does not destroy us ... will
probably turn into a Royal Commission."

ANYA

Very funny. You know, John A. had a few problems in his
own life. You and everybody think of him as this paragon
of privilege and success. The truth is he and his family
were immigrants that had to struggle to survive. For most
of his life he was barely able to financially support his
family. His brother and son ...

BOBBY

Blah blah blah. Cry me a river, White girl. Thousands ...
no, tens of thousands of our people died horrible deaths.
Several generations of families torn apart because of him.
Perspective and context. There's those words again.

ANYA

What an asshole! I guess you don't have to be from Parry
Sound to be one.

BOBBY

I have no idea what that means.

She looks over at Hugh, still by the
jukebox, obviously in his own little world.

ANYA

What about your buddy there – Hugh? Where does he
fit into this?

BOBBY

I brought him along for support. And he needs is to get off
the Rez occasionally to see the world.

ANYA

A graveyard in Kingston is not the world. You dragged
him along because you couldn't do this alone, am I right?
I'm right, aren't I? You somehow convinced him to be an
accessory to your crime. What a stupid shitty thing for a
friend to do.

BOBBY

I am his friend. Practically his only friend. You don't know
his family. They have issues.

ANYA

We all have family issues. I was raised on a dairy farm
and my father took it as a personal insult that I'm lactose
intolerant.

BOBBY
Yeah well, Hugh's family ... they have different ... priorities.

ANYA
What the hell does that mean?

BOBBY
Hugh is the middle child of seven. All quite successful and high-achieving, except for the dancing queen there. His three older siblings are literally a doctor, lawyer, Indian Chief. Most of his family don't really care for him. He's too different. They barely tolerate him.

ANYA
He seems perfectly fine to me.

BOBBY
You haven't listened to the way he talks? He's a throwback to another era. He's an aural and oral person. Most of us process stuff visually but when he hears something, it's implanted. Have you ever heard him do an accent? It's annoying but perfectly executed. Same with his thing with music. That's his reality. In another time and place, I think he would have been a master storyteller. Unfortunately, this world has little time for master storytellers.

ANYA
And so you thought the best thing was to drag him into this?

BOBBY
All master storytellers need a master story to tell. So, my colour-challenged friend, you gonna turn us in?

ANYA

One: bite me. Two: I'm not unsympathetic. First Nations
people have every right to be pissed off. To want to burn
bridges and blockade roads, I get that, but it doesn't mean
you actually have to. It's a metaphor.

BOBBY

Tell that to the people at Oka.

ANYA

I wasn't even born when Oka happened.

BOBBY

It still happened. I know well-educated, middle-class
White women have different priorities from ours. In fact,
those priorities are frequently the antithesis of ours. So it
would be really nice if you could reach deep into that
social guilt that quite probably throbs deep within you,
and forgive us our many trespasses.

ANYA

Wow. On the graph of assholes, you just like beating the
bell curve, don't you? Look, I am not going to apologize
for my race, my sex, or my upbringing. If I call the police,
it won't be out of racism. It will be because you're an
asshole and I know for a fact they exist in all cultures.
Thank you for proving that. Ah screw it. Do what you
want. I have reached my asshole quota for the day. Dig all
the way to China for all I care.

*She starts digging in her pockets for money
before realizing she doesn't have any.*

BOBBY
Oh. Would you like me to buy that beer, said the Indian to the White woman?

ANYA
Fuck you.

> ANYA storms out. HUGH notices her
> leave and comes running over.

HUGH
She left.

BOBBY
I see that high school diploma of yours was well-earned.

HUGH
You've really got to stop driving women away, Bobby. It's counterproductive.

BOBBY
This had nothing to do with Yvonne.

HUGH
Angry smart woman, hurrying away from you to the door in the middle of one of your escapades. I don't know, looks pretty familiar to me. I was getting to like her.

BOBBY
The day I accept girlfriend advice from you ... is the day you get a fucking girlfriend. Until then, shut up.

HUGH
I am so tired of this. I am so tired of you. To tell you the truth, I'm getting so goddamned exhausted cleaning up

after you. Of course something like this was going to happen. I ... you ... you oughta know better.

HUGH begins to sing louder and louder as his dream takes over the stage. Again, HUGH takes centre stage and begins singing at BOBBY, once again replacing "you" with "Hugh." It's Alanis Morissette's "You Oughta Know."

HUGH storms out of the bar, leaving BOBBY behind. SIR JOHN reappears, enjoying his cocktail.

SIR JOHN
I would argue Canada would not be Canada without what exists in this glass. I daresay Canada was conceived through the veil of numerous hangovers. The making of a country is not for the frail. It's for men who have vision, and brandy or gin can help focus that vision. God, try to imagine a nation created by temperates. Might as well leave it to the Indians.

People who complain about me, about my drinking, I tell them to go bugger themselves. Do you want to know why I drink? (*pause*) I drink ... The hell with it. It's as if God has burdened me. He has given me great tasks and elicited great payment. I carved this country out of rock, mosquitoes, and endless horizons. I see its potential. I know its greatness.

People place a little too much importance on my occasional indulgences. After all, I do not think I drink any more than any other Scotsman. My life is just a wee bit more public than most. Still, it gave me the fortitude to steer this country through the treacherous waters of

Confederation. And not just me, find me a politician who didn't drink ... and I'll show you a man who thought the Devil lay at the bottom of every glass. And logically, the best way to drown that Devil is keep him inundated by perpetual drink. (*raising his glass*) To Canada!

Lights down.

Act Two

SCENE ONE

*Once again, SIR JOHN is standing in front of a
huge map of Canada circa late-nineteenth century
(from sometime between Confederation and
SIR JOHN's death, in 1891), nursing a drink.*

SIR JOHN
To create a country, you must be an alchemist. Such an
operation can require a handful of diplomacy. Maybe a little
dash of blackmail at the right time. A pinch of vision and,
finally, a huge helping of hard work. And if the temperature
is right, and God is feeling benevolent that day, a new
country is born. The secret is ... you have to be able to see
what could be, not what is. Too many people with petty
concerns see only what is. They can't take that next step.

Frequently, for amusement and dare I say inspiration,
I read literature that deals with what could be. Jules
Verne, Mary Shelley, etc. Simple tales of and from those
who could see a little farther than the average man, and
can imagine the impossible. The world may be full of
visionaries but there can only be one vision when it came
to Canada. Mine.

He takes a drink.

SCENE TWO

*HUGH and an angry ANYA are walking
by the side of the road. HUGH tries to
keep up with the brisk-walking woman.*

HUGH

I can't leave you here. Look around, there's nothing for
kilometres.

ANYA

You think I'm gonna call the police ... That's why you don't
want to leave me here.

HUGH

No, I don't want to leave you here because there's nothing
around for kilometres. I know you think we're some
crazy Indians ...

ANYA

I never said "Indian."

HUGH

I'm sorry, a crazy NAFNIP. And we ...

ANYA

What the hell is a NAFNIP?

HUGH

Oh that's a Native Aboriginal First Nations Indigenous
person. NAFNIP. Didn't they teach you anything
in university? Look, it's dark and desolate out here.
Whatever you may think of us, we're not the type of

people that leave women on lonely deserted roads. Bad things can happen.

ANYA

No, you're the kind of people that desecrate graves and steals national treasures. Just vandals.

She storms away and HUGH races after her.

HUGH

No no no. Wait wait. You've got the wrong idea. There's this medicine bundle ...

ANYA

What is this medicine bundle you two keep talking about? Is it worth going to jail for?

HUGH

For Bobby it is. A medicine bundle is a collection of spiritual and sacred items, usually wrapped up in a deerskin. It belonged to Bobby's grandfather.

ANYA

You know, for him to be as screwed up as much as he seems, it would have to take generations.

HUGH

Anya, stop for a second. That medicine bundle was taken away from his grandfather when he went to residential school. Bobby was raised by his grandfather. His father ... Well, let's just say there were problems, serious ones, with his father. His mother lived with another guy who found Bobby annoying. See, you're not alone.

ANYA
Hugh, really …

HUGH
Almost done. His grandfather died seven months ago. And
he should have been buried with that medicine pouch.
He wanted to be buried with that pouch. Months of
prowling the internet and Bobby found it in a European
museum. It's been his goal to reunite the pouch with his
grandfather. Bobby promised.

ANYA
That's why you guys are on your way to Kingston? That
almost makes him sympathetic.

HUGH
I know. Right!

> *There is a moment of silence. Only the sounds
> of the nearby highway can be heard.*

ANYA
I think you're nuts for trying to pull this off but I've got
enough headaches on my plate as it is. Who am I to argue
with a sojourn of justice.

HUGH
Great, grand, groovy. Now, shall we continue our little
journey, or seriously, do you want to try your luck
hitchhiking on this dark and deserted road?

ANYA
Back to him? This day just gets worse and worse.
Okay, let's get going. The mosquitoes are almost as
annoying as him.

HUGH

Truer words were never spoken. Let's rock and roll. Anya! To the Hugh-mobile.

They walk toward the car.

SCENE THREE

They are driving again. This time, ANYA is in the front seat. There is tension.

ANYA

Hugh, did you know Macdonald's father and son were named Hugh?

HUGH

I did not know that. Tall, handsome, noble men?

ANYA

Uh I'm not sure. Sir John A.'s father, Hugh, was a poor businessman. The son, Hugh, after a long estrangement with his father, ended up both mayor of Winnipeg and briefly the premier of Manitoba. Passed some sort of temperance act.

HUGH

Well, I am currently in search of employment. But neither of those positions appeal to me.

BOBBY

Anya, here's a question for you: How much do you know about First Nations people? Overall.

ANYA

I've read a lot of Thomas King.

BOBBY

Everybody's read Tom King. The raccoon that lives under my house has read Tom King.

ANYA

So what then? Do you want to know if I've been to any pow wows, Bobby? First Nation communities? Stuff like that?

BOBBY

I just think it's a shame that people like you, a typical young Canadian of Caucasian persuasion – I say that respectfully – knows more about a guy that's been dead for over a hundred years than the people sitting in the car right next to her.

HUGH

Give her a break, Bobby. I'm sure she knows lots. She's in university. What are you taking, by the way?

ANYA

Prozac, mostly. Look, I know about the same as most other Canadians my age would. Maybe a little more, maybe a little less. What ... do you wanna quiz me?

BOBBY

Yeah, why not? What are the Seven Grandfather teachings?

HUGH

Oh come on, Bobby, even I can't name them all off by heart, just like that.

BOBBY
That's why I am not asking you. Anya?

ANYA
Wait a minute. I saw this on a T-shirt once. Bravery,
wisdom, honesty ... strength ...?

HUGH
Let's hear you name them ...

BOBBY
Shut up. Anya, name seven First Nation communities.
There are over six hundred but feel free to pick any.

HUGH
Bobby ...

ANYA
No, it's fine. Let's see. Six Nations. Rama. Tyendinaga.
Akwesasne. Cape Croker ...

BOBBY
Technically it's now called Chippewas of Nawash, but I'll
accept that. That's five. Two more.

ANYA
I don't know ... that ... that Oka place!

BOBBY
I'll have to give you a half point for that one. Oka is
actually the name of the nearby White town ...

HUGH
(*in French accent*) And a very tasty cheese, if I do
say so myself.

BOBBY
The actual name of the Native community is Kanesatake.

ANYA
And what exactly does this prove?

BOBBY
That the Canadian educational system deems it more important to teach kids about an ancient dead racist alcoholic than about the approximately one million people of Indigenous decent that are walking, and driving, these lands today.

ANYA
I know people like you, Bobby.

BOBBY
You do?

ANYA
Yeah, I have a lot of gay friends.

BOBBY
What?!

HUGH
Ooh, this should be interesting.

ANYA
Like with any marginalized culture, for a few of them, everything they perceive or experience is a comment on, a reflection of, or as you say, is filtered through their sexual preference. They can find it difficult or even uninteresting to relate to anybody outside that bubble. I have a feeling with you, if it's not Native or related to it, you're not that

interested. Happens with a lot of people who have strong socio-political leanings. Take feminism, for example.

BOBBY
Do I have to?

ANYA
Yes. I'm a feminist but you get a group of feminists in a room and sometimes it's pay equity this, patriarchy that, till it's intersectionality and gender parity coming out your ass. All important issues, yes, but sometimes you just want to sit around drinking a glass of wine and insulting your ex.

BOBBY
I take it you are referring to the rarefied world of North American dominant culture feminism?

ANYA
I'm sorry. You plan to comment on feminist theory?

BOBBY
Who? Me? Never. However, it's been my experience that the feminism you espouse is overly preoccupied with equality and representation, but on occasion they can lose focus of the fact there are different priorities, depending on the people or the place.

ANYA
Yes, I've heard this argument before and, believe it or not, I agree. Last month, I was at a Black Lives Matter rally. I realize this is me saying this but I do understand that for a Black woman, it's more important for her son or brother to come home, not shot by a cop, than to make more than minimum wage or have equal representation at the board table. It's a much broader perspective. I know I'm lecturing

to the converted here ... I mean Iroquoian women and
their matriarchal culture ...

BOBBY

We're not Haudenosaunee. I hate squash.

HUGH

Both the sport and the vegetable.

ANYA

... could teach contemporary feminists I know a
thing or two.

BOBBY

The whole concept of leading by not visibly leading. Darn
clever, those Haudenosaunee, squash or no squash. See,
Native feminism has a different feel and priority to it. Case
in point – a bunch of us guys would go visit my cousin,
Sheila. She has a house right on the water. Beautiful on a
hot sunny day. Occasionally one of us would ask her to get
us a beer, and she would.

HUGH

You couldn't get your own?

ANYA

No no no no. Don't fall into his rhetorical trap. I've
noticed. That's what he likes to do. As Sun Tzu says, don't
fight the same enemy too many times or he ... or she ...
will learn all your battle tactics.

HUGH

I will remember that ... if I ever bump into this Sun Tzu.

BOBBY
My point is, by the end of the afternoon, she'd gotten
us maybe three beer each. Eventually, my cousin Todd
looked around at her yard and said it looked like the grass
needed cutting. So he offered to cut it for her, right then
and there. A grand total of maybe ten minutes of getting
beer versus two hours of cutting grass in the hot sun. It's
her own form of female empowerment.

ANYA
I'm not sure what Naomi Wolf would say about that but,
again, you've just made my point. You're back to filtering
everything through that Aboriginal lens. If it's non-Native,
you don't care.

HUGH
That was your point?

BOBBY
It's all interrelated. And I do like a lot of non-Native stuff.

ANYA
Uh huh.

BOBBY
(*sullenly*) Star Trek. Hockey. Cowboy boots ...

ANYA
Look, it's getting really late. I realize you two are wannabe
grave robbers ...

HUGH/BOBBY
Wannabes?!

ANYA

... and full-on wacky. But if you want, you guys can crash at my place.

HUGH

That sounds good. I'm sold.

ANYA

Maybe a good night's sleep will snap you back to reality. My roommates are away for the week and I've got two couches. You can do your sojourn of justice thing in the morning. And I make mean lactose-free pancakes.

BOBBY

(*still giving list*) Air conditioning. Bikinis.

ANYA

You know, the last twenty-four hours ...

HUGH

Yes ...

ANYA

Broken hearts and stolen graves ...

HUGH

Sounds like another country song.

ANYA

Speaking of which, feel like some music?

HUGH

Always.

ANYA turns on the radio. At first, everybody begins nodding their head in beat to the song, as HUGH, once again, exchanges the realism of the car for being a rock star. He pulls a wireless mic from his jacket. This time he's singing "Nothing Compares 2 U" as sung by Sinéad O'Connor, again replacing most of the "you"s with "Hugh"s.

At some point ANYA joins him in singing.

SCENE FOUR

SIR JOHN in his office. Once again there is the big map. He is pointing at Manitoba.

SIR JOHN
Louis Riel had a vision I suppose. Most madmen do.
If Canada were to have a devil, his name would be Louis Riel, this so-called Father of Manitoba. He vexed me.
He vexed me so. He could not see past his own backyard.
The needs of Canada were more important than his Half-Breeds. His rebellion, the death of Scott ... His lunacy ...
The man actually petitioned the Pope himself to relocate the Vatican to the new promised land. The promised land of Manitoba! What kind of sane man does that?! This man ... he ... Did I mention how much he vexed me!
Luckily he was more of a visionary than a skilled diplomat or a student of warfare. It was only distance that provided him any measure of advantage. If you ask me, he was Canada's Frankenstein's monster, cobbled together from the worst bits and pieces of French and Indian parts;

an insane monster set out on the world to inflict havoc those he hated, and pain his Creator. He had to be hunted down and dealt with, as was the monster in the book.

His accursed vision cost this country dearly – the financial expenditure to deal with him, the ugly publicity from his cursed shenanigans, and political fallout from his death. I am widely quoted as saying: "He shall die though every dog in Quebec bark in his favour." He did hang, and they did bark. And they are still barking. I think they mourn the symbol, not necessarily the man. It's amazing how one demented Half-Breed can so disrupt a country dedicated to peace, order, and good government. Hopefully, as the years go by, his name will fade into the obscurity of history and the accursed actions he is the author of will no longer be mentioned. One can only hope and pray.

> SIR JOHN exits. ANYA's apartment. All
> are sitting on a various chairs and a
> couch around a coffee table. On the coffee
> table in front of them is an open pizza
> box. They are all sharing the pizza.

ANYA
… and he really knew how to make an entrance. At an early conference exploring Confederation, he showed up in Charlottetown with something like thirteen thousand dollars' worth of champagne to impress all the political leaders. And it worked. Say what you will, the man knew how to work a crowd.

BOBBY
I bought your beer. I bought the pizza. But I don't buy that.

HUGH
Ah, Kingston, you can just smell the history ...
metaphorically. (*politely*) Your house smells very nice.

ANYA
Better than a farm. Macdonald had no choice coming here
as a five-year-old but as he grew up, he always came back.
This was his home.

HUGH
(*really into ANYA*) That's fascinating.

BOBBY
I told you all this stuff already, on our way down here.

HUGH
Yeah but I like it better when she tells it.

ANYA
Oh you're a sweetie. Okay, let me get you some blankets
and pillows. Back in a second.

> *She exits.*

HUGH
I'm a sweetie.

BOBBY
Hugh, what are we doing here? This wasn't part of the
plan. Let's get out of here.

HUGH
Leave? Yvonne ... That's it. She reminds you of Yvonne,
doesn't she?

BOBBY

She does not. No. Yvonne was taller. And heavier.
And Native.

HUGH

And would stand up to you, talk back to you, test you.

BOBBY

This has nothing to do with Yvonne.

HUGH

I think you like her. You do, don't you?

BOBBY

Me? Hell no. She's opinionated, loud, pushy ...

HUGH

Right. That's the antithesis of you.

BOBBY

This is not about Yvonne.

> *ANYA enters carrying a mismatching
> bunch of blankets and pillows.*

ANYA

Who's Yvonne?

HUGH

Hey Bobby, she wants to know who Yvonne is.

BOBBY

Well, that is fascinating. Good for her. It's not important.

HUGH
That's a matter of perspective. Anya, let me tell you a story. Yvonne was a smart, beautiful woman, a cousin of mine, and former girlfriend of Bobby, who currently is going to university in Peterborough. Working on her Ph.D. in Indigenous Studies. When we passed the 115, I thought for sure the car was going to veer right.

BOBBY
He's exaggerating. She's just an old ex-girlfriend.

HUGH
Right and *Star Wars* was "just" a movie. The problem is she found Bobby's choice of in-your-face lifestyle a little counterproductive to a solid education. You've seen Bobby at his best and worst. Imagine that for eight years. See, a good chunk of the Native population are getting educated these days. Formal education is now referred to as "the new buffalo."

ANYA
"The new buffalo"?!

HUGH
Yeah, because it will provide for all our needs. It's an Indigenous metaphor.

ANYA
The new buffalo. Got it.

BOBBY
I hate that term. Historically, not everybody existed off the buffalo. It's culturally myopic.

HUGH

Bobby would prefer "the new pickerel" or maybe "the new muskrat" for the Ojibway.

BOBBY

Anishnawbe. Christ, I wish you'd use the right term.

HUGH

I got tired of trying to teach White people how to say "Anishnawbe." After a while I started pronouncing it wrong "Ojibway/Anishnawbe" – "tomato/tomato" … "Ojibway" is easier in mixed company.

BOBBY

It's still wrong. That pizza was salty. Got anything to drink?

ANYA

Let me think … In the fridge there should be some beer, soda water, Diet Pepsi. Oh and maybe a Snapple.

BOBBY

Ooh, a Snapple.

ANYA

Hugh? (*nodding eagerly*) Be right back. But keep talking.

BOBBY

Really? Does he have to?

ANYA

Yes, he does. My house. My rules. It's a Caucasian thing.

ANYA exits.

HUGH

(*louder*) It's the classic story. I'm sure you've heard variations of it. Boy meets girl who's living with another guy. Boy becomes their best friend. Other guy breaks up with girl and moves away. Boy ends up dating girl. Boy ends up dragging her to too many protests and marches. Boy can't understand why she doesn't find pissing people off together as romantic as he does.

ANYA

(*off-screen*) Imagine that!

HUGH

After her fifth Public Mischief charge, girl opts for a more sedate life of making a difference to her people through embracing "the new buffalo." Girl moves away. Boy decides to dig up a politician's grave. I'm sure that story line has been explored in a dozen movies.

ANYA enters carrying three Snapples.

ANYA

That's why he's so pissy to me?

BOBBY

I am not pissy to you. Hugh, you talk too much.

HUGH

Only because there's so much to say. You can always call her, you know. Talk.

BOBBY

I did.

HUGH
You did? And?

BOBBY
I shouldn't have called. There wasn't any reason. We were
just repeating ourselves.

ANYA
And here you are doing exactly what split you two up.

BOBBY
That's because I am who I am. And there are larger,
meaner problems in the world that eat up little problems
like Yvonne's and mine.

HUGH
The "hill of beans" argument.

BOBBY
Those are still the more important battles.

ANYA
Not the kind of thing a girl wants to hear.

BOBBY
Some tell people what they want to hear. Others tell them
what they need to hear.

ANYA
And then there's Chris, who told me neither.

BOBBY
Who's Chris?

HUGH
The asshole in Parry Sound.

ANYA
We just broke up. That's why I was at the McDonald's.
About twenty minutes before we met I had been in the
washroom crying my eyes out. Sometimes a girl just wants
and needs to hear something positive.

BOBBY
Sometimes guys too.

There is an awkward silence. ANYA
quickly starts making up the couches.

BOBBY
Okay then, I think we should go.

ANYA
You sure?

BOBBY
We'd better. You must be exhausted ... Hugh.

HUGH
I guess that grave is not going to dig itself.

All three walk to the door.

BOBBY
Thanks for everything, Anya. It's been ... educational.

ANYA
Same here, Bobby.

HUGH

It was truly a pleasure to meet you. I wish you the best of
luck in whatever you find yourself doing.

ANYA

Keep singing.

HUGH

How can I not? There's no word in the Anishnawbe
language for "goodbye." Only, "I'll be seeing you."

ANYA

That's almost romantic. I'd say stay out of trouble but …
Oh Hugh, I think this is yours. Thanks.

She tosses the bear spray to him.

HUGH

No problem. Bears of Kingston, beware.

BOBBY

Hugh, let's go.

She closes the door behind them. They exit.

SCENE FIVE

*It is late in the night. A deserted
graveyard. HUGH and BOBBY enter,
carrying shovels, a crowbar, flashlights,
a tourist map, and a big duffle bag.*

HUGH

Well, she was nice. Sure we couldn't stay?

BOBBY

No. She was ... distracting.

HUGH

You know, I was thinking, if we dug up all the Fathers of
Confederation and stitched them together, we'd have a ...
Franken ... father ... Or a "Frankenfederation."

BOBBY

Goddamn it Hugh, keep your voice down. This is serious.

HUGH

You're a little too serious. I think you need your own
happy place.

BOBBY

I don't want to sing.

HUGH

That's my happy place. All it is is a place you can go where
you can do what you've wanted to. Where you check your
logic and reality at the door.

BOBBY

Doesn't sound like me. I prefer my logic and reality
with me at all times. Now my map says it's over here.
Cataraqui Cemetery.

HUGH

Sounds Iroquoian.

*They walk up to the gravesite. They study
it for a moment, before HUGH kneels
down and reads the gravestone. Slowly.*

HUGH

"Father of Confederation. John A. Macdonald. 1815–1891."

BOBBY

Seventy-six years. He lived seventy-six years. Three years longer than my grandfather.

HUGH

Not much of a tombstone. Somehow I was expecting something bigger.

BOBBY lifts his shovel. HUGH grabs his arm.

HUGH

Wait, I think I see somebody coming.

BOBBY

It's dark. Those are shadows. Come on.

HUGH

Bobby, this is ridiculous. Look at us. We aren't very good grave robbers. You even brought me the wrong kind of shovel.

*He holds up a flat-edged shovel, not the
pointed tooth-shaped one BOBBY is carrying.*

BOBBY

A poor workman blames his tools. Our cause is just.

HUGH
You're trying to tell me this is some sort of hallowed
shovel of justice?

BOBBY
Yes. Very. What we are doing is a fair and measured
response to an outrageous imposition. They have, over the
years, taken our children, they have taken our dead, they
have attempted to take everything.

HUGH
The medicine bundle. Remember that? I thought that's
why we were here.

BOBBY
That was implied.

HUGH
So here we stand, in a cemetery in the middle of the night,
about to dig up a bunch of bones. And hold them for
ransom to get back that medicine bundle. Doesn't that
seem a bit contradictory to you?

BOBBY
Are you backing out now?

HUGH
Friends don't let friends dig up dead prime ministers.
I came to support you, to support your grandfather. But
there's nothing quite like standing in the middle of a
graveyard at two in the morning to give you a reality
check. Everything your grandfather taught me – us –
if you broke something, fix it. If you took something,
replace it. It wasn't about punishment. It was about
maintaining a sense of balance. I don't think this is

restoring balance and harmony. This is more along the line of revenge and revenge is never a good path to follow.

BOBBY thinks for a moment.

BOBBY
But my promise ... Goddamn it, Hugh!

HUGH
Hey man, all this stuff is stuff your grandfather taught us. If you don't care about what I'm saying, you don't care about what your grandfather said.

BOBBY
Goddamn it ...

With a nod, HUGH exits the stage. BOBBY walks over to the grave. He stands before it, struggling with what's going through his mind.

BOBBY
Hey. Mr. Macdonald. I bring you greetings from the Anishnawbe people. They wanted me to tell you, they are still alive, despite everything.

Angrily, he shoves the spade into the grave. It remains standing as he paces, gathering his thoughts.

My buddy Hugh tells me a happy place is where you can do what you want, express what's in you. See this shovel, boy would I like to ...

SIR JOHN appears, startling BOBBY.

SIR JOHN
Easy with that shovel, lad. You could hurt someone.

BOBBY
What?! Oh fuck ... Shit ...! (*yelling*) Hugh!!

SIR JOHN
(*looking around*) What an odd and dark place. And you ...
Who are you?

BOBBY
Bobby ... Bobby Rabbit.

SIR JOHN
An equally peculiar name. And Mr. Rabbit, I don't
believe we have ever met, and I have an excellent
memory for faces. And your face ... even in this light,
seems a tad darker, more exotic. You wouldn't be from
one of the Mediterranean races, would you? Perhaps
Italian or Spanish?

BOBBY
I am Anishnawbe.

SIR JOHN
And what, pray tell, is that? Something from the
Caribbean perhaps.

BOBBY
Ojibway.

SIR JOHN
Ojibway?! You're an Indian?!

BOBBY

A rose by any other name ...

SIR JOHN

An Indian who knows his Shakespeare! Will wonders
never cease.

BOBBY

Grade eleven English. Got a B plus on it.

SIR JOHN

I have no idea what that means. But you seem to be
doing well for yourself. You speak English well, and look
very ... civilized.

BOBBY

I will try not to take that personally. Still, I want to punch
you right in the middle of that big red nose of yours.

SIR JOHN

Have I offended you, sir?

BOBBY

Yes sir, you have. In so many ways. Do I look like a happy
Indian? No, I am one severely pissed off First Nations man.

SIR JOHN

But I don't understand. I am a friend to the Indian man.
I used to sing in a Mohawk choir when I was young.
Everything I and my government have done has been for
the eventual benefit of the Indians of Canada.

BOBBY

Eventual benefit?! You starved us.

SIR JOHN
Starved?! No, that is a gross misjudgment of the situation.
You have to understand how government works. It's
complex. But the need to relocate the majority of Indians
to Reserves became increasingly necessary. Unfortunately,
as with the management of any large group of people,
many did not see the benefits of what we were trying to
provide and, well, it seemed the most prudent way to
encourage the recalcitrant into seeing the wisdom of our
ways. Spare the rod and spoil the child, I suppose. It could
be conceived as harsh, true, but in the end –

BOBBY
In the end, you starved them into submission.

SIR JOHN
I am the Prime Minister of Canada. I must do what I can
to make sure this country operates and grows. I wouldn't
expect you to understand but it was for the better
good of Canada. There were migrants looking for land.
Canada needed a population. A population that would
do magnificent things with the land. Indians have no
knowledge of the importance of the rich land they used
simply to shit upon. You Indians have no respect for the
law. And Canada is a nation of laws. If they did not want
to live on the Reserves we negotiated, then they must deal
with the repercussions. Yes, some went hungry. We all
have been hungry. Coming across the ocean as a child,
we were fed a gruel that … Well, I frequently chose to go
hungry. I could see beyond the grumbling of my stomach.
Indians can't seem to do that. What are you here to
whine about?

BOBBY

I want my grandfather's existence on Mother Earth to be acknowledged. I want my grandfather's experiences at residential school validated. I want how my father turned out … to be understood. I want the world to appreciate how important, how vital my grandfather's medicine bundle is and where it should rightfully be. With him. Not in a museum. Same with ten thousand other equally important Aboriginal items. And I want to know that for all my yelling, all the angry things I've done in my life, something good will have come from it. And I can close my eyes for a while.

SIR JOHN

Well spoken, lad. You can thank me for the ability to make a speech like that. And just what is this medicine bundle? One of your superstitious contrivances?

BOBBY

First of all, bite me. Secondly, it was something my grandfather held close and treasured. He felt it was the essence of who he was and who his people were.

SIR JOHN

And I have it?

BOBBY

You set the sequences of events in motion that ended with my grandfather in a residential school, the bundle ending up in a far-off museum, and me standing here in the middle of a cemetery.

SIR JOHN

Son, on any given day, I deal with a thousand requests from a thousand people all wanting something. And you think your little medicine bundle is worthy of my time? You want my advice young man ... learn to plow. That will do your people more good than this hocus-pocus. Now if you will excuse me, I am a busy man.

BOBBY
One quick question. I have always wanted to know this from you. Just coldly and simply. What makes you so sure your way of life is better than ours? You and your people have tried so hard to change us, civilize us. Why?

SIR JOHN
Because that's what we do. Yes, we complicate and justify it by couching it in decrees and religion and laws. You want an explanation for everything people do, good luck son. You're going to have a long time waiting.

BOBBY
That's not a very enlightening answer.

SIR JOHN
You want enlightenment, light a candle.

BOBBY
What about my grandfather's medicine bundle?

SIR JOHN
What would you have me do, Mr. Rabbit? Go knocking on the museum doors myself saying, "Give me all your Indian medicine bundles I've got an irate Indian barkin' up my ass"? I think not.

BOBBY
I hadn't thought of that. (*pause*) That might work.

SIR JOHN
What are you talking about now?

BOBBY
(*to himself, working an idea out*) What if I did go over there?
Right to the museum, to all the museums, and petitioned
them directly. Right on their doorstep. Right? I mean, yeah,
it's easy to ignore somebody when there's an ocean between
you. But if I go there, right in their face, they've got to listen
to me. I'll take the fight directly to them. It would be a
public relations nightmare if they didn't listen to me.

SIR JOHN
I suppose. I went over to England and came back with a
new country. And a knighthood. Also, as I remember, the
food was substantially better on that trip.

BOBBY
Well, that was the important thing, wasn't it? Hey, wanna
hear something funny? My grandfather was named John.
He didn't create much of anything worthwhile, other
than my family. And nobody's throwing him a party. You
broke so many things about my people and it's going to
take us generations to fix. But we will. We are survivors.
We survived small pox and tuberculosis. We survived the
Indian Act. We survived you.

> BOBBY *turns away. SIR JOHN*
> *exits. ANYA enters.*

BOBBY
(*pause*) Europe ... I should go there.

ANYA
You're going to Europe? Wow, a lot can change in an hour.

ANYA *startles* BOBBY, *who screams,*
startling ANYA. *They both jump.*

BOBBY
Goddamn it!

ANYA
Geez!!! What?

BOBBY
Sorry. Anya, what are you doing here?

ANYA
I couldn't sleep. I was curious, you know, about your
sojourn of justice. I wanted to see if you actually ... did ...
what you said you were going to do. So ...?

BOBBY
Wanna buy a shovel? Never been used.

ANYA
What happened?

BOBBY
The purpose of a medicine bundle is to bring out the best
in a person. And I'm standing in a cemetery at two in the
morning about to dig up the grave of Canada's first prime
minister. You might notice the inherent contradiction. It's
late. You probably have classes tomorrow ...

ANYA
Yeah ... no. I don't go to university. I used to but ... that's
another story. I work at Bellevue House. Sir John A.'s old
home. He lived there for a year and a half. I dress up in a
period costume and tell tourists all about the man. Surprise.

BOBBY

Why didn't you tell us?

ANYA

It's a little embarrassing, having dropped out and all. I plan to go back. So what now? I mean for you and Hugh?

BOBBY

I'm going to Europe.

ANYA

That should be interesting. For both you and Europe. Where's Hugh?

BOBBY

Probably off in his happy place. I have a really sucky happy place. I think Hugh has a crush on you.

ANYA

Really? That's too bad.

BOBBY

You don't like him.

ANYA

Oh he's cute and adorable, but I, on the other hand, bat for the other team.

BOBBY

You ...? (*realization*) Chris?

ANYA

Christine. I probably should have mentioned that before but sometimes telling strangers that can make them uncomfortable.

BOBBY
I always seem to be readjusting my perspective of you.

ANYA
Hey, just think of me as a broken-hearted lactose
intolerant lesbian who dresses up as a nineteenth-century
charwoman for a job. I'm living the dream. Let's go find
Hugh and go to my place. Bobby, I will say it's a pity you
weren't born a woman.

BOBBY
You know, I get that a lot.

They start walking away.

ANYA
By the way, I read somewhere that important graves
like this one, they're like surrounded by a couple feet of
cement. To protect them.

BOBBY
WHAT?!

They exit.

SCENE SIX

— —

*HUGH is by himself on stage, looking
out at the audience. He speaks.*

HUGH

Off into the darkness they walk, and the lights come down
on our grand tale. And what of Anya? Has this chance
encounter made her overcome her distaste of male penes?
(*shaking his head no*) And Bobby, will he travel across
the vast ocean and butt heads with the great museums
of Europe, resulting in several very public and nasty
international incidents, the final product being a new phrase
he learns: "forced deportation"? (*nodding his head yes*) And
what of our true hero, the brave and handsome Hugh, what
happens to him? Will he find happiness? Will he find a
job? Will he ever end up centre stage at the National Arts
Centre? Well, that's … that's a story for another night.

SCENE SEVEN

*HUGH is once again in rock-star
mode, this time with Cheap Trick's 1977
hit "I Want You to Want Me" – still
singing "you" instead of "Hugh."*

At one point ANYA and BOBBY join in.

*Finally SIR JOHN joins them
on stage. ALL sing.*

END OF PLAY

ACKNOWLEDGMENTS

Sir John A: Acts of a Gentrified Ojibway Rebellion was the result of an alchemy of ingredients and inspirations, all of whom I would like to thank in helping me write this. First and foremost, Jillian Keiley, the National Arts Centre's English Theatre Artistic Director. Ms. Keiley, I am sending you a high five ... what the hell, let's make it a high six. And of course my fabulous cast – I'm talking about you, Herbie Barnes, Darrell Dennis, Katie Ryerson, and the amazing Martin Julien. All made a play about Canada's first prime minister something to sing and dance about.

Jim Millan, the legend. He and I matured during the 1990s Toronto theatre scene together, but never met. We even hung out at the same restaurant/bar back then and now. Twenty years later, he sculpted my play into something nobody was expecting and I believe everybody who saw it loved. Thanks, Jim. Truly a pleasure to work with you.

A special thanks to Ed Roy who provided me with some well-needed and well-considered dramaturgy and advice.

A play like this, a historical drama (regardless of the humour and pop music infused into it) relies heavily on accurate history and facts. I actually had to employ substantial elements of the R-word – "research." I read Richard Gwyn's two volumes of biography of John A. Macdonald, respectively titled *John A.: The Man Who Made Us; The Life and Times of John A. Macdonald, Volume One: 1815–1867*, and *Nation Maker: Sir John A. Macdonald; His Life, Our Times, Volume Two: 1867–1891* (Toronto: Vintage Canada, 2008 and 2012). As well, I devoured *Canada Transformed:*

The Speeches of Sir John A. Macdonald, edited by Sarah Katherine Gibson and Arthur Milnes (Toronto: McClelland & Stewart, 2014). Also interesting was James Laxer's book, *Staking Claims to a Continent: John A. Macdonald, Abraham Lincoln, Jefferson Davis, and the Making of North America* (Toronto: House of Anansi Press, 2016). And finally, for something different, I also read *Sir John's Table: The Culinary Life and Times of Canada's First Prime Minister*, by Lindy Mechefske (Fredericton, NB: Goose Lane Editions, 2015). I now know how to make nineteenth-century shortbread!

A phenomenal thanks to Martin, Katie, Darrel, and Herbie ... my dream cast. This play was so much fun to do, partly because I got to work with these people. I will never listen to "I Want You to Want Me" again without seeing all four belt it out. Same with the so-called "behind the scenes" people, who were very much present and accounted when I watched everything happen on stage.

And, of course, a huge and amazing *chi-miigwech* to the lovely and talented musical artists who created the songs of my youth, never suspecting they might someday get used in a Canadian–Indigenous play.

To my mother and Janine. Two women without whom it would be difficult to create anything.

DREW HAYDEN TAYLOR is an award-winning playwright, novelist, essayist, and filmmaker. Born on the Curve Lake First Nation in Central Ontario, Drew has done practically everything from performing stand-up comedy at the John F. Kennedy Center for the Performing Arts in Washington, D.C., to serving as artistic director for Canada's premiere Indigenous theatre company, Native Earth Performing Arts, in Toronto. Somehow in the midst of that, he's managed to carve out time to write the occasional story. *Sir John A: Acts of a Gentrified Ojibway Rebellion* is his thirty-first book.

Photograph: Thomas King